WHAT IS LOVE?

QUESTIONS A CHILD ASKS

WRITTEN BY DAR DRAPER

ILLUSTRATED BY SARAH DAWN HELSER

D1307020

Dedicated
To the memory and inspiration
Of "Sweet Mr. Drye,"
a man who loved children
and knew the Answer
to "What Is Love?"

WHAT IS LOVE?

COPYRIGHT © 2004 BY DAR DRAPER

ALL RIGHTS RESERVED.

PRINTED IN CHINA.

ISBN 0-9740880-4-8

PUBLISHED BY

LIFEBRIDGE
K I D S

P.O. BOX 49428

CHARLOTTE, NC 28277

Presented to:

_____

With Love,

_____

Date:

_____

What is love?

What does it look like?

Can I see it?

Can I find it?

What is love?
What does it *feel* like?
Can I touch it?
Can I buy it?

What is love?

What does it taste like?

Can I bake it?

Can I eat it?

What is love?

What does it smell like?

Can I sniff it?

Can I breathe it?

What is love?

What does it sound like?

Can I hear it?

Can I scream it?

And where is love?
Where does it come from?

When is love?
When should I get some?

Why is there love?
Why do we need it?

Who is love?
How can I meet it?

So many questions
For someone your size!
Let's discover Love's "Who"
"What" "Where" "When" and "Whys."
Your sight, touch and taste
Might give us a clue.
Sweet smells and loud sounds
Will help us out too....

We see love in smiles
Of people we know.
Love shines in bright eyes
And makes faces glow.
Look right beside you
And there you will find
Love looks like your neighbor
Who is helpful and kind.

Love can be felt,

Like hugs from a friend,

Or a tender sweet kiss

When the day's at its end.

You can't really touch it,

But love can touch you...

You never can buy it!

It's free when it's true!

Sure, love can be tasted

Like cookies and cake,

Or after school snacks

That your mommy may bake.

But love's not the cookie —

It's the heart that went in

To please and refresh you...

Love's why she made them!

Love smells like the scents
Of places you know
Like Grandmother's house
Where you love to go!
Sweet treats and fun memories
Fill up the air!
You can breathe in that love —
It's everywhere!

Love sounds like laughter
Or clapping hands
When you've hit a home run
And hear cheers from the stands!
Of course love is heard
In words everyday...
You can scream it or shout it
And give love away!

Love can be found
All around and inside.
You always can get it
For love never hides.
We need love because
There's a place in our heart
That only love fits...
It's the big missing part.

Love's part can be filled
By Someone Who lives!
True Love's name is God —
From His hand He gives

All the love that we need,
All the love that we share.

His love is amazing,
And nothing compares!

We all have felt love
In one way or another,
But when we meet God
We know love like no other!
To find Him is easy
Just ask Him to come.
Then you will have love —
And Who it comes from!

You'll see it and feel it
And taste it and breathe...
You'll hear it and shout it,
"I know what love means!"